Words of Life Vol. 1: Works of Christian Poetry

By Patrick Henry

All Scripture quotations, unless otherwise stated, are from the King James Version of The Bible.

3P: PH Pentecostal Publishing, LLC
New Albany, OH
3p-phpentecostalpublishing.weebly.com

Contents

Preface

The title of this collection of poetry was taken from a Bible verse: Philippians 2:16 (KJV). In this verse, the Apostle Paul admonishes the Philippian church to "hold forth the word of life". The term "word" in this verse is rendered from the Greek term "logos" which refers to the Divine expression of a living mind. Logos is used in John 1:1, 14 to refer to Jesus Christ Himself: the Word of God. Thus "word of life" refers to the foundational Word of God as embodied in Jesus. Paul exhorts this church, and by extension the body of Christ throughout this era, to proclaim the Word of life. Through this book, it has been my aim to continue to fulfill my duty to respond to Paul's call by proclaiming biblical truth via poetry.

A major aspect of proclaiming the Word of life is faith, for the Word of God declares that the just live by faith (Habakkuk 2:4; Romans 1:17). In other words, it is only through responding to God's Word with a heart of faith, fully trusting in Him to perform all of His promises, that we can enjoy the abundant life characterized by peace, love, and joy. For faith counteracts fear – which is the root of anxiety – and unbelief, both of which erode our peace and joy and, more generally, diminish our quality of life. Thus, the cover of this book portrays the simple yet profound word of faith spoken by Jesus Himself in Matthew 21:21.

You will notice that I utilize Bible verses throughout the poetry contained in this volume. Some of the poems in this volume have words and/or Bible verses written in smaller font beneath the title of the poem and above the actual poem text. I do this as a means of providing some background information concerning the poem, or, in the case of Scriptures, I do it to offer a way to introduce the poem. I have borrowed this method from the book of Psalms in the Bible. Thus, before reading a poem with such an introduction it might help to look up the Bible verse(s) mentioned prior to a particular poem in order to gain a deeper understanding of the poem. Similarly, you will notice Bible verses to the right of particular lines of some poems; these Bible verses are meant to provide a Scriptural basis for the main point of the particular line of poetry with which it is paired.

PS - The Prologue of this book is a poem that succinctly describes why I write poetry. All bible verses listed in this volume are from the King James version, unless otherwise noted.

May God bless you richly. Enjoy!

Minister Patrick Henry, M.A., M.A., LPC

Prologue:
My Hope for Poetry

i write

words
wonderful words
wrought within

recollections
reminiscent of
winters & warm-seasons
once were, once-again

one writes words remarking upon
weeks-gone
weeks-now
weeks-next
ringing of revelations remarkable...
one-Lord oneness
one-Faith
one-Baptism
one-Love
one-Salvation won...derful

when Jesus relates words,

i write

JESUS Is...

Lamb of God (John 1:36)
Lion of the tribe of Judah (Revelation 5:5)
the Holy One and the Just (Acts 3:14)
Shepherd and Bishop of your souls (I Peter 2:25)
captain of their salvation (Hebrews 2:10)
great high priest (Hebrews 4:14)
door of the sheep (John 10:7)
the way, the truth, and the life (John 14:6)
Prince of life (Acts 3:15)
advocate with the Father (I John 2:1)
Wonderful (Isaiah 9:6)
Prince of Peace (Isaiah 9:6)
I AM THAT I AM (Exodus 3:14)
Immanuel (Isaiah 7:14)
faithful witness (Revelation 1:5)
good shepherd (John 10:11)
bread of life (John 6:35)
living water (John 4:10-14)
love (I John 4:8)
heir of all things (Hebrews 1:2)
the Almighty (Revelation 1:8)
Ancient of days (Daniel 7:9)
Holy One of Israel (II Kings 19:22)
Counselor (Isaiah 9:6)
light of the world (John 8:12)
resurrection and the life (John 11:25)
true vine (John 15:1)
man of sorrows (Isaiah 53:3)
everlasting Father (Isaiah 9:6)
author and finisher of our faith (Hebrews 12:2)

Branch (Isaiah 11:1)
root and offspring of David (Revelation 22:16)
The Word of God (Revelation 19:13)
Faithful and True (Revelation 19:11)
Sun of righteousness (Malachi 4:2)
mediator of a better covenant (Hebrews 8:6)
the Lord, which is, and which was, and which is to
come (Revelation 1:8)
Jehovah-jireh (Genesis 22:14)
Jehovah-nissi (Exodus 17:15)
Jehovah-shalom (Judges 6:23-24)
Jehovah-tsidkenu (Jeremiah 23:6)
Jehovah-rapha (Exodus 15:26)
Jehovah-shammah (Ezekiel 48:35)
Jehovah-raah (Psalm 23:1)
Alpha and Omega (Revelation 1:8)
the beginning and the end (Revelation 22:13)
the bright and morning star (Revelation 22:16)
Apostle and High Priest of our profession (Hebrews 3:1)
the only Potentate (I Timothy 6:15)
Son of man (Matthew 8:20)
King of kings and Lord of lords (Revelation 19:16)
Son of God...In other words, (Matthew 16:16)
Jesus is God. (Isaiah 9:6, I John 5:20; John 10:30)

God's Right Hand Man

His right hand man is the Son of Man
All Power in His hand, power to snatch
Man from the misery of sin. Your beginning
Is where you begin but His right hand
Stretches further than that in time past
Hovering over righteous men long past-
Jacob, Isaac, Abraham and his lass back
To the firstborn son, Adam whom God formed
With the same hand that He might have
An object with which to share His image
And to which He did extend His hand over
And over again…He regretted His plan
To become a family Man as man ran away
From Him towards his wicked desires.
Killers, fornicators, adulterers, and liars;
Haters, hypocrites, general misfits
Populated the earth. Fast forward past Noah,
Moses, Joshua, the great prophets of old.
We see that God loved these leaders, though
His people Israel were so cold toward Him,
Fickle even. They would cease from their sin
Only for a season, creating the reason
For God to send His Son so that the price
Of sin man would not have to pay, for Christ's
Death on the cross took that reproach away.
And His resurrection paved the Way for Maker
And man to have loving fellowship again.
If you only have faith and follow God's
Plan - baptism, repentance, holiness - and feel
His Spirit fill you within to remove the taste

For sin from a human once a foolish man
Afterwards a tongue-talking saint redeemed
By the Hand of the GodMan Jesus,
The Lord Incarnate: God's Right Hand Man

HOLY SPIRIT

Oh blessed paradox.
In one SUPER-natural episode,
You descended upon them-
The 11 that believed
& many others-
in a flurry of flames
that did not burn.
Deliverance...to all at once
out of confusion – Understanding;
out of wandering — Direction;
out of pain — Healing;
out of deceit — Truth;
out of chaos – Peace
out of weakness — Power
out of death—
...Life

a rebirth
for though we are birthed of the flesh,
You shall be "born of water,
and the Spirit (John 3:5),"
says
He-
The Son
Speaking of His Spirit,
The loyal Intercessor,
Litigating to His Father on our behalf
Through tongues unknown to the speakers,
yet clear to Him from whence they came.
Who is this One (there's no trinity)?

The great Helper & Teacher;
The Spirit of Christ Jesus
To be clearer,
I speak of The Holy Spirit
I pray that this Spirit fully fills you.
In Jesus' name
Amen.

Jesus the **SonLight**

The SonLight looks @ His sons and sees His
reflection
The Light makes your beauty manifest is His
confession
With a twinkle in His eye, He made this profession,
"I want man in glory with Me…
with at least one concession.
There was one predestined to fall,
Judas, son of perdition.
Please do not follow him.
He chose not the Light,
Went left and not right.
He rejected My Love
Like a fool
And heaped up his treasures on earth, not in the
heavens
Broke My heart
But he had to go, he was the leaven

Within the group
Who after Me did follow.
And kept their eyes on the Light.
In the darkness they did not wallow
But strove for what was right
In My sight
not theirs.
For their faithfulness I brought them upstairs
To where I stay
Though very different were they
The 12 of whom I speak to thee –

A lawyer, fisherman, later a Pharisee –

And today's saints
You, though one, differ too…
Really it is obvious
Next to my bosom are you
And for you
I advocate, like a lobbyist
Of My blood you've tasted.
My afflictions you share
For you have I died 'n risen, that eternity you might
share
So chubby, bow-legged, short/long hair
As a loving Father, why should I care?
Into My Light you've come in,
And became the same
Having Power to bind demons, to heal the lame

So please My children by creation see
I AM no respector of persons
My heart yearns for fellowship with the unsaved
The black, white, yellow, and red-skins
The prostitute, killer… mankind…with all his sins
Whatever ear that will hear, I'll welcome him in

To the magnificence of My Light:
Which is My glory and instruction in Truth
Out of the abundance of My mercies and grace
I'll save the old men, middle age, and the youth
The learned and ignorant, thirsty men of every race

For they that hunger and thirst after righteousness
shall be filled…
With My Spirit, which is Light
That the radiance of My Light might shine forth
through you,
To condemn the wicked and to draw the humble
Into My family, which are those who obey My
will."

In tears you cry out, 'To become your kin, what
shall I do?"
"Repent and be baptized in my name. And I, Jesus
Christ the SonLight, will dwell in you!"

LoIAMve

(I am in love with Jesus, and He's in love with me.)

like a man's soul, of sin's cost bereft (Romans 4:8)
like your beloved's scent lingers after she left

like summer wind, without image or direction, only
felt
like Sonshine poured down, to the skin- warmth; to
the heart help (Malachi 4:2)

like a Father in the eyes of His infant Son
like the tune of a hymn just begun, "angelic" voice
sung (Ephesians 5:19)
(hear Ken sing a song)

like a heart-swell that overwhelms your being, at
the sound of "Jesus" –
(pause)

like when He makes your mountains plains
like when He brings forth the latter rain
like when, for His fame, He keeps you sane, and/or
heals your pain
with the blood that once flowed from His veins

like when you close your eyes, behold the hole in
His side,
the Son of Man crucified (Luke 23:33)
the Lamb who removed your sin (John 1:29)
and for you He died (Romans 5:8)

Like when you watch yourself become less like you
were
and more like you ought to be,
Displaying spiritual maturity,
all because He got in thee.
Please pay attention and
see…

like when God Himself
not placing running Creation on hold
enters your abode
to say,

"I AM…with you (friend).
I AM…healing you (healer).
I AM…delivering you (deliverer).
I AM…answering you (counselor).
I AM…sustaining you (sustainer).
I AM…leading, teaching you (teacher).
I AM…in love with you (lover, like none other).

I AM in creation and beyond creation
Yet simultaneously I AM ALL these things for you
For I AM…" (Exodus 3:14; John 8:56-58)

That's what it's like…and more
When He -
When Jesus -
Knocks on your door
(Pause)
And you open…

Love

Love is…
Lifting your heart to praise your God
Though your bills outnumber your money
And that sickness just won't go away
And your children won't obey

Love is…
What's left
When warm feelings and glad tidings
have forsaken you;
when faces are bereft of smiles
and tears have become your friends
and when part of you yearns for the end
of this life, and the start of the next

Love
Of your God
Love of your Jesus
Is what remains
It's what keeps you, anchors you
When all else fails

Love
Is what guides you
When the day is picturesque
Even when the storm rages

It gently nudges you
Beckoning you
To manifest the light of Christ

In a dark world

It encourages you,
"Though you can't always see it,
The Son is still shining!" Love says

Love
Wakes you up early for prayer
Even though it knows you'll soon fall asleep

Love was there
When God, by wisdom, created man

Love was there
When God covered their sin after the Fall

Love was there,
When Abraham, by love of God, obeyed and
prepared to offer Isaac

Love was there
When you forgave your spouse for hurling darts at
your heart

Love was there
When you wondered how anyone could love you
In affirmation, it whispered, "Jesus does!"

And what more shall I say?
For the time would fail me to elaborate on how
love:

BELIEVES ALL THINGS
BEARS ALL THINGS
HOPES ALL THINGS
AND ENDURES ALL THINGS

Love never fails you
Because God is Love!

The Oasis of Praise

Nehemiah 8:10 …for the joy of the Lord is your strength.

Psalm 33:1 - Rejoice in the Lord, O ye righteous: for praise is comely for the upright.

Psalm 100:4 - Enter into his gates with thanksgiving, and into his courts with praise: be thankful unto him and bless his name.

Isaiah 26:3 - Thou wilt keep him in perfect peace whose mind is stayed on thee: because he trusteth in thee.

There are times
When it seems that
Circumstances
Have gotten the best of me
And in turn
brought out the worst in me
when I have little mind
to hear
encouragement,
let alone to encourage myself
when the term *frustration*
seems to only
scratch the surface
of what I am feeling…
I've wandered into a desert land

BUT
When
I
Think
Of the goodness
Of
Jesus

And ALLLL
He's done – and, by faith, will do – for me…
I am translated
So to speak
Up and out of my situation
And into an oasis of praise
The life-giving place in a dry land
In the natural nothing has changed
but
In the Spirit
I've broken loose from my troubles
Like an escaped slave
Leaving them behind
And entered in…
Focused on Christ is my mind
And there peace resides
I praise
I praise
I praise
His holy name
I raise holy hands
And lift a thankful heart up to heaven

My soul leaps into the oasis of praise
And recollections flood my mind
"If it had not been for the Lord…
I woulda been cut off
On my way to a devil's hell
A Christless grave
I woulda been, still in a psychiatric ward
Tormented and grieved…"
And as the memories keep pouring in

My soul overflows with praises unto the Most High
And a wave of joy sets in,
my God
Sweet joy

So although I'm still in the desert
Though my circumstances have not changed
I stand firm
Refreshed, renewed in strength
Sustained by the oasis of praise

This
Is the aim

This
Is the goal

That when my drought comes
I raise holy hands, lift up a thankful heart, and
Draw in a clear mind

And enter in
To the OASIS of PRAISE

Praise Unlimited

Inside any child of God
Within their very being
Reaching the depths of the spirit
and stirring the soul
There is a bottomless well
A well of praise

Have you tapped into your well?
Does your cup runneth over?

If not…
Remember, just remember
Let the memories flood your mind
And stir the well-water of praise

Recall how the Lord drew you,
Courting you as an assertive suitor

Think about…
How Jesus saved your soul from sin
How Jesus kept you all these years
How Jesus provided for your every need
How you lost your mind
And you were even suspicious of your closest
friends
Running in fear from those who sought to help you
BUT God…for Jesus restored you to your right
mind

That was me…but maybe you…

…had a mind to leave church
And become tangled again in the bondage of sin
You had one foot out the door
The other barely held the door open
And to the pastor's warning you gave a deaf ear;
to the minister's plea a hard heart
you alllllllllmost…BUT somehow, someway
Jesus restrained you from leaving

How Jesus
consoled you,
loved you,
comforted you,
clothed you,
fed you,
protected you

Remember…what's your testimony?
Reach the recesses of your mind
For through memory we plunge into our well of
praise
Thus stirring the waters thereof
For every recollection
Of the wondrous works
Jesus has wrought in our lives
We dive deeper,
deeper,
deeper
Sinking into the
sweet waters of gratitude
the life-giving streams of thanksgiving

passing from praise to praise
then you praised for His performance, now for His
person
then for His works, now for His wonder
then for His actions, now for your praise
then for His hand, now for His heart…

and the waters stir and roll, rise and fall
with such a tumult and vigor that surpasses anything
natural
(its supernatural)
it crescendos until…the Spirit retrieves another
testimony
from the vaults of your mind
and the stirring continues; time and space seem to
fade away…

welcome to praise unlimited

<u>Undone</u>

Acts 2:1-4, 13-17

I am the priest.
I am the living sacrifice…
As is my praise,
Offering them up to God
I come undone.

Worship…
involves sacrifice,
discarding all thoughts and behavior
having not Him as the epicenter.
forsaking etiquette
appropriateness
appearances
self-consciousness
and what I think others are thinking.
Losing myself in Jesus,
I come undone.

For only when I forget myself,
And focus on God
Can I hope to enter in.

Otherwise,
I am tightly wound up
In cognitions and metacognitions,
Distractions,
As a caterpillar in a cocoon

But when it comes undone

It dies.
In that it ceases to exist in one form,
Only to live again in another.
Freedom.

Likewise,
only when I,
yea when we,
come undone
can we make a sacrifice
pleasing unto the Lord.
we die to ourselves
and
with a pure singularity of focus
bask in life in His presence…
a foretaste of heavenly bliss.

Come undone.

We Are One

Our God is one God. Saints are in Jesus. We (saints and believing Jews) are one in Him (see Ephesians 5:30; Romans 11:12-20).

We are One
Just as He is One –
Father, Son, and Spirit –
One in Christ.
Likewise we are made in His image –
spirit, soul, body –
one in man

Separately:
He creates…we create
He procreates…we procreate.

But together,
in the Spirit,
all children of Abraham
are one in Him –
in Jesus.

We are His flesh and His bones.
We do what He did
on the earth:
He healed…we heal;
He cast out…we cast out;
He rebuked storms…we rebuke storms;
He raised the dead…we raise the dead.
We do it in Jesus. Jesus did it through God.
Our signs – wrought through the Spirit.

Jesus' signs – wrought through the same.
Jesus laid the foundation; we build thereon.
Jesus set the pattern; we follow it.
Jesus paved the way; we walk in it.
Why?

Because saints serve Jesus,
as Jesus served the Father.
This is our duty.
For all that Christ did,
we must do as well.
His ministry must continue in our own
His ministry & ours…
since there is discrepancy between the two,
Let us go higher
& deeper…
let us pray as He prayed,
fast as He fasted,
study as He studied,
love as He loved…
for in Adam we are made in His image;
but through rebirth we are remade in His image
spiritually
Always in Christ
For WE ARE ONE.

POWER

Power to heal
Power to bind
Power to yield
Power to cast mountains into water with words
Power to create action with verbs
Power to dispel spirits unclean
Power to commune with the Holiest Being
Unseen

Power to lay hands
Power to stand
Withstand
Stand with
Power to share my brother's burden - "It's my shift"

Power to raise the dead
Proclaim death dead
Power to overcome sin
Power to prove the truth of the Word
Said of Him
By Him
It's Him
Power to deem atheism absurd

Power to live
Power (to self) to die
Power from on high
Power the same
as when the Spirit first came
in tongue-flames

and they preached His name
Power of JESUS…

Let it reign
It must reign
It shall reign
Praise His Name

The Battle is Won (Taken)

Taken
Snatched
Out of the hands of the enemy
Then I was an enemy of Christ
Now I preach the cross
And the resurrection
Of Jesus –the Christ
Whom the prophets foretold should come

It is He that has removed the darkness
And given me light
Who has taken my bonds
And made me free
Who has taken my crooked path
And made it straight
Who has taken my blindness
And caused me to see
Who has seen my weakness
And He is now my strength

Yes
Christ has saved me
Jesus won the biggest battle of them all:
The battle for my soul
He put Himself on my mind
Through His grace – dispensed with one hand
In the other, His mercy
That gave me life
When I deserved death
Though I was in sin

He gave me the revelations:
1. lustful was I
2. I was far from Him
3. more of Him I did need
and thanks be to God, I obeyed
to the salvation of my soul

so
I am taken
Wholly captured
Christ has me
No longer do I serve the enemy
The battle has been won
He has overcome Satan
In my life
And ended the strife
Between He and me
So that I can Rest In Peace
When this life is done
And the next begun
As long as I hold onto the Son
Again I say, the battle is won

Trust Not In Yourself

Trust not in yourself
But trust in Him who is able
To take the gainsaying out of your friend's mouth
To cause your father to treat you right
To make your worst enemies give unto you
Both money and materials
And be at peace with you

For our God is sovereign
And nothing is beyond His power to perform
He is a Man of war
Who will fight your battles
He will cause the flood waters in your life to cease
For He has set the bounds for their flow
And make rivers in your desert
He'll be the lily of your valley
Yes He will
He'll literally prepare a table before you
in the presence of your enemies
And cause you to triumph
Like Joshua at Jericho

You only gave Him faith
And obedience to His Word
He did the rest
Defeating your enemies
Or winning them over
Lighting the Way
That your steps might be ordered
Providing for needs

So that you never want for bread
Saving your soul, progressively
That sin has no hold on you

For all of these reasons
And many more
Trust not in yourself
But trust in the One Who made it ALL
And governs it ALL
Who can do anything but fail
No matter the heights you reach in this life
Remember, we are His creation, His servants
So when everything is on the line
or when nothing is,
at all times
Trust not in yourself…but trust in Jesus

I Run

Know ye not that they which run in a race run all, but one receiveth the prize? So run, that ye may obtain. And every man that striveth for the mastery is temperate in all things. Now they do it to obtain a corruptible crown; but we an incorruptible. I therefore so run, not as uncertainly; so fight I, not as one that beateth the air: (I Corinthians 9:24-26)

I run
Not too fast
For wisdom says, "Slow down, son."
Not too slow
For I'll be left behind
a decent pace, step-for-step with Christ
Steady
A step ahead of my foe

I run
Not for sport
Or leisure.
No,
Rather
This
Is
My
Vocation,
My calling.
To take up my cross
Deny myself
And follow my Lord
On to glory!

I run
Not to win
But because I've won
Thus,
I run
In triumph
[Jesus has beaten my foe]
Telling myself, "Just endure.
Finish the race.
And you'll have overcome."

I run
I have set my face like a flint
And fixed my heart
My mind is made up
Running
Forward
Is
The
Only
Way

So I run.
Though the battle rages on
And I've been wounded by the enemy
Though the way is shrouded at times by fog and
trees
And even my old nature fights against me
Yet, I strive;
Yet, I press;
Yet, I praise;
Yet, I pray;

Yet, I love;
Yet, I study;
Yet, I believe –
Bringing my flesh
Under subjection
[Let it serve me
Not vice-versa].

And by His grace
Through my faith
I SHALL OBTAIN
That crown
And life eternal:
Fellowship with the Father

I run.

Apprehended, In Order to Apprehend

Not as though I had already attained, either were already perfect: but I follow after, if that I may apprehend that for which also I am apprehended of Christ Jesus. Brethren, I count not myself to have apprehended: but this one thing I do, forgetting those things which are behind, and reaching forth unto those things which are before, I press toward the mark for the prize of the high calling of God in Christ Jesus (Philippians 3:12-14).

Caught
Trapped
In the most positive sense

I am apprehended
Grasped
By the arms of my Savior

Hold me tight Lord

Funny
Now that You have me
I want to have You
The way You have me

And this is what You desire
My sweet Jesus
For me to earnestly seek Your heart
Not just Your hand
To know Your character
Not just Your blessings

So
I've been apprehended
In order that I might apprehend

I've been caught
In order that I might catch
You
To know You
and the power of Your resurrection
And the fellowship of Your sufferings
Because before honor is humility

So let it be done unto me, oh Lord
That I may learn of You
Through experience
Through tests and trials
Through revelation
For truly my soul thirsts after you
I long for Your Word
Your touch
Your presence
Like a warm fire
On a cold winter's day

Or like the smile of my beloved
After a job well done

Come Lord Jesus
Come to me
As I come after You
Now
And

forever

Hallelujah

The Will of Man

The will of man
Can be strong and
Unyielding, like quicksand

As it sucks you in
The wrong path you have chosen
Let the trouble begin

For you see
A man's ways are right in his own eyes
But the end thereof is death
Not the kind with a coffin
But the kind where you're coughing
From all the smoke
Caused by all the burning and fire
Of the place where you'll spend eternity
Separated from He – the Father, Son, Spirit –
The ONE GOD, Jesus (there's no trinity!)

Yes, the will of man
Apart from salvation's plan
Can have a man
Outside of God's will
Because the will of the unsaved man
Is driven by his own selfish desires
Not by the desires of God

So what of the saved man?
He too has a will
And towards the desires of the flesh is it bent

a war ensues – flesh vs. Spirit
the aim is that the will be rent
from its marriage to desires and lusts
that draw God's ire
and wed to the all-perfect plan
of the God-Man
Jesus
Who desires to conform Christians to His image
(Romans 8:29)
to the saving of their soul

This prize is one
that can only be won
Through prayer, fasting, the Word, determination
And above all love for Him, which brings
obedience to His Word
Plus
The help of the same friends that helped you get
saved:
Repentance, humility, and desperation
Because for Him to work in you
Both to will and to do
Of His good pleasure
We must
1.Humbly know that without His Spirit leading us
we will go wrong
2.repent when our will is not in tune with His
3.be desperate to reject our ungodly desires and
embrace God's will, which will lead to eternal life

so saint of God
say to your will, say to your flesh

"Yes I know you are strong
but you will not steer me wrong
to Christ's will you must bow
as revealed in His Word, so now
you must obey
I command you this day
And will rebuke you again
If you entice me to sin
For I count Jesus as my Friend,
My God, my Lord
And with Him I desire to be on one accord
So let the heavens record
That for Christ I live
And for Christ I will die
I use my will power to obey Him
And with Him will I comply."

Will Power

Will the blows continue to fall?
Or will you stand up?
Will your posture remain bent?
Or will your back stiffen?
Will the tears continue to run?
Or will you dry your eyes?
Will time flee your futile grasp?
Or will carpe diem prevail?
Will your voice remain mute?
Or will it boom and echo with a resounding volume,
reaching the heavens and shaking hell…

Will you…
Stretch out your hand,
Push aside the symptoms of prejudice, racism, and
hate
That plague *our* Human Body
And befriend your fellow man,
Though he may be many shades darker,
blue-eyed, or Spanish-speaking?

Will you…
Lift up your right foot,
Then your left.
And through your
perseverance,
intelligence,
foresight,
compassion,
and faith-

Through your leadership-
march to the forefront of this generation?

Will you...
Cast aside base desires,
and temptations, of your own creation-
Pleasures inherently good
But morally anachronistic-
Thus presently immoral
Though widely popular,
Unwilling to accept these...
as uncontrollable tendencies...
Remember: 'To exercise proper dominion over
creation,
You need to have dominion over you.'

Will you...
Hold your head high
And daily celebrate your heritage-
Whether you're a son of Masinissa, Caesar, Khan,
or Ivan;
Readily rejecting the day's cultural imperialism
That ironically threatens to bind you
Hand and foot
To the misery of psychological, cultural,
moral, and developmental indentured servitude?
They say:

Here, you can wear those, what do you call them?
Yeah you can wear those 'cornrows' when you play
ball,
I know you're gonna cut your hair,

like everybody else,
for that job interview…

Will you be for the truth,
When it's more *deadly* than the lie?

Will you be ashamed of your God,
Or will you openly love Him
With all your mind
And with all your heart,
And with all your soul…?

Will you *fill the unforgiving minute*
with 60 seconds worth of distance run…

Will you seek your potential,
And not the security of *sufficiency,*
Or the calm of complacency?

Will you smile?
Will you pray
Will you grow?
Will you,
Could you,
Won't you
Say
*I love you…*to everyone
And mean it?

sun Rays, Son Raise, sons Raise

sun rays
Bathe me in Your warmth
Energize me
Touch my spirit
Through Him that is within
me,
By flesh – son of man
By Spirit – son of the Son;
Him, the only begotten
1st born
1st Risen

Who inaugurated a new day
For the sons of men
Revealing and being the Way
For these sons to rise
From the depths of darkness
When the sun's rays,
Though far off,
Found us

Like they found Israel (Ezekiel 16:4-6)
An infant,
Unclean,
½ dead,
wallowing in its own blood
umbilical uncut

YES
The Son's rays poured down upon us also

Us, yielded to the small sun within
Lifting our heads up
Unto the risen Son
We've received His Rays,
His Essence,
Poured forth,
His life-giving Power,
Yea, even His Spirit.

For as the sun's rays shower vegetation
And catalyze the motions of life
So do His Rays,
His Spirit,
Quicken our spirit-
That of the fallen sons of Adam
The 1st- created
Whose eyes left the face of the Sun
And thus they perceived darkness
Now apart from the risen Sun,
In this black place is where we,
Heirs of Adam, reside

Until…
My Lord
Until
The dawn breaks
With every crack of the whip
With every punch of the fist
With every thorn in His head
Every nail in His body
Every drop of His pure blood that fell…
Our darkness waned

And BEHOLD a new day!
As the Son broke forth
Risen again,
As He was 3 days before
Now with all power, healing
In His wings

BEHOLD, the Lamb of God
Who takes away the sins of the world.

This Lamb is the Son
& the Son is Jesus
of which the sun you see is a physical symbol
the sun, whose rays
give sight, warmth, psychological health
Rays of hope, rays of faith, rays of love, rays of
life…

My friend
Won't you receive His Rays?
Won't you receive the Son's Spirit?
The Holy Spirit of Jesus
Won't you pray with me

I need Your Rays,
dear Son of God.
I need Your Spirit.
Rain on me
That I may rise
As you have.
That these sons of men may rise
And turn our faces unto the majesty of a New Day

In Zion

In Jesus name
Amen

The Underdog

"I chose you not because you were great in
number," God said
And this is true indeed.
For our Lord did not set His love and favor on the
mightiest people
No
Rather He took lone Abram,
A pagan by birth
And from his loins and from a dead womb,
created a people – yea even a nation, even a race –
for Himself

A people whose sheer number and might
Was solely derived from their peculiar ties to their
God:
Israel
A nation mighty
Because their God is mighty
A nation great
Because their God is great
Undefeated in war
Whenever they remained faithful to their God
Though their foes were great and many
Yet before God's chosen people they could not
stand
For Jehovah Nissi fought for Israel

God demonstrated His power and love
By choosing to use an underdog, often-backsliding
people

To reveal Himself to the world
God, out of His love, espoused Himself to Israel
And with tenacity keeps the bond
Their rebellion reveals His mercy
Their longevity reveals His faithfulness
Their apostasy reveals His steadfastness
Their weakness reveals His strength
Their preservation reveals His hope

A hope available now to all mankind
Through the work of Christ
For in Him,
Yea even His body
Are combined the Jew and Gentile believer
By faith in Jesus
We are all one body
One Lord. One faith. One Baptism.
But it all began
Because God chose
The underdog

Pour Out My Heart

Psalm 62:8

Surrounded by people
yet all by myself
pretty girls all around
but I can't date any of them

I'm a fish out of water
a 30-something Black, husband
in a world of single, 20-something white females

an Apostolic, in a sea of so-called Protestants,
athiests, Catholics, and relativists

what have I gotten myself into!

These hear my voice more than my wife and kids

there is little relief
only a longing...
an expectation

seeing my family...everyday

graduation
job
healing
reconciliation

when, Lord? When?

On one hand Time runs swiftly
on the other it can't run fast enough
my busy-ness turns days into minutes

But

the separation turns those same days into years

even so...Come Lord Jesus

for part of me would rather be with You
than make my way through
but my 2nd mind wants to see my end
our end
what end?
When we are together
husband & wife-
with 6 degrees between us-
parents and children

restoration of all things lost...
or broken in our lives

then I'll be surrounded by people
and intimately connected to them all
in the midst of a pretty woman
who happens to be my wife

a fish back amongst his school
safe
secure
Home

Sometimes (The Weather)

Sometimes
I can't see the sun
Try as I might
It is nowhere to be found

But
Somehow
I know it's there

Sometimes
I can't feel the sun
Try as I might
It is nowhere to be found
But
Somehow
I know it's there
Because the laws tell me
The sun will keep shining
Though I cannot see or feel it

Sometimes
I can't feel the Son
Try as I might
He's nowhere to be found
But
Somehow
I believe He's there
Because the Word tells me
He'll never leave

He'll always shine upon me
Filling me with His light, warmth
I need it
I need Him
I need Jesus
To fill me with His light, His warmth, His Spirit
Over
And over
And over
Again
That out from me
Would flow the light, the warmth, the power of God
That true Sonlight

The Future as Pre/sent
(the courtship)

I can taste very well
I can *taste* her gaze
I can *taste* her smile
I can *taste* her shape
I can *taste* her laugh
I can *taste* her scent
I can *taste* her touch
I can taste…her love

These figurative palette-pleasures
All wrapped neatly
In my hearthoughts
A present
Existing in the past
Experienced in part now
Expected in the future

Which I can taste too
This time to come
Is on the tip of my tongue
Or on the end of the horizon
Where the Sun, through her, melted the ice
that covered my heart
which now beats frantically
in response to her…the present

tantalizing
titillating
the taste buds

that anticipation mounts
within me
I become
a child on the eve of Christmas
when we give good gifts
as the Father gave to us
Himself
The greatest Gift
Life forever
For all willing recipients
of this
Present,
pre-sent
By God

As was she
My present
Pre-sent
To inhabit like spaces/places/times
In recent past
Where I was
For she desired
To make the appointment
He had set for our meeting
Then only an interlude
Next for a lifetime
Will be our present
In the future

She and I…Presents
Pre-sent
To one another

In the past,
No, from the beginning
Was it decreed
And I can taste it
I can taste His Words
Spoken then and NOW
The Light
Whose intensity in my eyes grows
A beacon
Leading me to our chosen time
Hers and mine
Which is past
And also which will come

Leaving the present bittersweet
But the bitter only makes the sweet sweeter
And as the future for us
Becomes
our present
The sweetness OVERWHELMS my taste
So that even that which was once bitter
Becomes
Sweet

Like His Word
"Oh taste and see that the Lord is good;
Blessed is the man
Who trusts in Him!"

I will taste
I will trust
I will see

I will love
As our future
Becomes our present…

Why I Love You
(The Proposal)

Because you smile at me…and my heart swells
Because you confide only in me…and I covet the
privilege
Because you can minister to me…and I am
strengthened
Because you desire my heart…and I could not
withhold it from you

Because you are beautiful in every way…and it
weakens me
Because you arouse every aspect of my
being…effortlessly

Because I rejoice inwardly at your scent
Because you draw me as the moon draws the tide,
and the tide the sand
Without a flip of your hand
Through your hair
Or nearby to stand
 in my eyes u stare
Rather your presence alone captures me
Or by a vivid thought of you am I ensnared,

bound to you

Like Adam to Eve
Like Abraham to Sara
Like Jacob to Rachel
Like Christ to His church…

Because you, being pregnant with my promise, help
me fulfill it
Because you = a desire manifested…to me a tree of
life
Because you are holy, through Him
And pray for Him manifested through me,
To a greater degree
my spiritual maturity

Because at times you love me more than I love
myself…and would court suffering to prevent my
own

I love you because these ways you impact me-
Through your beauty, love, and spirituality-
Declare your value
(A price) far exceeding
The cost of any
Gift bought, time spent, sacrifice made

I love you
Because it flows naturally through me –
The only man-vessel fit for this task-
aided by His Spirit

I LOVE you, because He plus thee strengthens me
So will you take this ring
and promise to be
Mrs. Henry?

Why I Love You, II
(the anniversary)

Because of your smile
Your smell
And the swell
In your breasts
That takes my breath.
Because during this year
we have shared
(to which none other can compare)
You have been there.
Through valleys and plains
And all manner of terrain,
You love me the same.
I thank you.
Because of the strength you exhibit in times of
adversity.
Because despite my failings you are to me:
The Friend, lover, teacher, preacher, wife
extraordinaire
I need you to be.
And I thank you.

Because you have far exceeded my estimation of
your worth
enduring immense pain that you might birth
our first born. And again I thank you
Because with you I laugh, with you I play, with you
I cry, with you I pray.
I love you for reasons mere words cannot convey.
And to you this day I say, "Thank You."

One Day
(the promise)

One day…you'll be happy you married me
One day…just wait you'll see

One day…your days will be filled with pleasure
A quality union you'll treasure
When I'll turn your frown upside down
And there will be gladness all around
You'll have a heart filled with peace
And rest in sweet serenity

One day…I'll be prophet, provider, protector, and
priest
One day…your discontent will cease

One day…you'll go into the store and shop to your
heart's content
Giving little attention to the money that's spent
You'll have all that you desire
Except that which draws God's ire

One day…the promised future will be the present

One day…join in faith with me
One day…I'll be what I was meant to be
One day…just keep praying for me

One day…just wait you'll see
One day…

Return To Love

(Charity)Beareth all things, believeth all things, hopeth all things, endureth all things (I Corinthians 13:7)

To whom much is given
Much is required
And we have been given much,
This love we share
A gift from God
Though the fire may have dwindled
Becoming a small flicker of light
Let us strengthen that which remains
Spark a match
And ignite our passion

How?

Love believes all things
So
Let
Us
Believe
Believe we can rekindle that flame
Believe we can find what was lost
Believe we can redirect what has gone astray
Believe He can restore, rejuvenate
Me
You
Us
Believe in the power of love
And let it guide us
Let forgiveness and mercy be our allies

Longsuffering: our companion
anger, malice: our foes

Let us say to each other…
"I love you"
Through our ups and downs…
"I love you"
Though we fall short at times…
"I love you"
When the sky seems like it's falling,
And our world is crumbling,
And we seem so far apart…
"I love you"…and let us mean it

Let us *desire* one another…
As we did when we made our vows
Time: let us not fill it all with busy-ness
But spend some together

My sweetpea,
My honey,
my wife
my love,
Let us return to love

Words For the Husband *About His Wife*
(...to husbands in holiness)

To Lead...
Examine yourself
Be the change you wish to see in her
Let His Power be felt through your influence

Use: Love & Prayer;
Mercy & Truth
(There are no substitutes!)

Trust... in His method, not your own
After you have planted Word-seeds of Life
"WAIT, I say on the Lord" to bring the increase –
the growth in your Mrs. which He has given you to
desire,
for you, Mr., have delighted in Him

Speak less, speak Life
Criticize SPARINGLY and in love
For her emotions are on her sleeve
Instead intercede, add FAITH to your prayers
And The Sun of righteousness will nourish her,
your Flower will blossom!

Suffer long
Be not weary in well doing

Love her as Jesus loves you
And - if she submits to Him -
she WILL LOVE YOU in return-

She will happily follow your lead

Because You're Sovereign

Because You're sovereign, I can hope
I can set my sight on the impossible
I can fix my mind on the unthinkable

For the plans You have for me, none can stop
And the Way You have made for me, none can
block
I need only to endure and follow You
To receive blessings in this life
And the end of my faith – even life eternal

God, You stand above all
High and lifted up,
You reign over all Your creation,
both the good and the evil.
Since I am Yours,
and You are mine,
what shall I fear?
I am the son of the Maker and Sustainer of all
things.
Therefore, I echo the sentiment of the Apostle:
If God be for me, who can be against me?
Thus, I rest in You.
I am confident,
sure,
and resolute
in what You can perform through me
With my faith,
I reach for the dreams that don't make sense,
For the calling on my life -

A future state beyond the scope of my present view;
Beyond logic;
Beyond common sense.
Yet I hold to it,
With clenched fists.
I believe You will bring the calling, the dreams
to fruition…

It has already begun,
in spite of demonic attacks and
my own flaws.
Because You are sovereign!

Ain't it Funny?

Ain't it funny…
That we sit in chairs
With no thought of falling?

Ain't it funny…
That we never question
The image that- from the mirror-
Stares back @ us?

Ain't it funny…
That any 2 people see the
Same rose in different shades of red…
And both call it "red"?

Ain't it funny…
That the chair could break
But we BELIEVE it's solid…
That the mirror could be skewed
Yet we BELIEVE it reflects
Our image…
That our sensual perceptions are approximations
Yet we BELIEVE they're fact?

Ain't it funny…
That we put faith
In the sensual, the temporal
And call it "FACT"
But question belief in God, the Eternal
Calling it "FAITH"
When it's true

That facts like man will rot
But the Lord Jesus (Christ) changeth not

Aint it funny…

Faith **Is...**

Faith is... the currency between you and God.
You give Him faith,
He gives you blessings.

Faith is... what causes you to step out of the boat,
as Peter did,
And do the impossible.

Faith is... what brings healing
When you lay hands on the sick.

Faith is... what causes you to claim that new car as
yours,
even though your credit score is poor, and your
money is funny.

Faith is... what causes you to say, "It's already
done"
When you know it's His will.
Even though you have no idea how or when.

Faith is... what you lean on
When reason says, "No"
When logic says, "Not a chance"
And when man's wisdom says, "Can't be done."

Faith is... that spark that,
With proper attention and some wood,
Grows into an intelligent flame
Consuming all doubt

Faith is… an aspect of God's love.

Faith is… the fraternal twin of hope.
Hope says "It can happen."
Faith says, "It will happen!"

Faith is…the pair of glasses
Through which saints are to *see* reality;
Causing us to perfect ourselves,
Since we *see* heaven on the horizon

Faith is…
"**F**ully
Accepting
Insight
Through
Him"

Faith is…
Seeing without eyes
Knowing without rational thought
And walking without steps.

Faith is…

By Faith

By faith
Lay hold onto
Your destiny
As ordained by God (not by you!)

By faith
The child of God sets in motion
A chain of events that brings blessings to pass

For true faith causes you to work together with Him
to bring about your blessing:
Health, spiritual and natural prosperity
Are part of Jesus' will for the saints

But faith must live in your heart
before this future promise becomes a present
blessing

By faith we lay hold onto the blessings of God
in the spirit,
for at the present we have not the blessings,
then they are manifested in the natural
(we believe we have the blessing – we receive it, we
embrace it-   BEFORE we get blessed)

Faith in the Word of God –
as written in the Scriptures or as delivered by God
Himself-
pleases God and moves Him to act on your behalf
In order to do that which He promises to do

By faith imitate our Father
And speak those things which are not as though
they were…

By faith…I'm not weak; I'm strong
By faith…I'm not poor; I'm rich
By faith…I'm not dumb; I'm wise
By faith…I'm not sick, I'm healed
By faith…I'm not single; I'm married
By faith…I'm not jobless, I'm employed

By faith…we cause Him to open doors no man can
shut
By faith…we loose God's hands to do exploits
By faith…we gain access to the abundant life

By faith, By faith, By faith, By faith, By faith

THE JUST SHALL LIVE BY FAITH…

By Faith #2: Faith & Spring

For we walk by faith, and not by sight. (II Corinthians 5:7). These all died in faith, not having received the promises, but having seen them afar off, and were persuaded of them, and embraced them, and confessed that they were strangers and pilgrims on the earth. (Hebrews 11:13). Genesis 4 and Hebrews 11 lets us know that blood can speak. Well if blood speaks, then faith sees. "How?" you say. Well, if we walk by faith and not by sight then we are NOT moving through life being led primarily by what we perceive with our senses or even what we think. Rather, we move through life based upon the Word of God- both the Bible and whatever God speaks to our spirit in prayer (which will NEVER contradict the Bible). Our faith in His Word causes us to see by faith. For example, we see that we're healed even though the symptoms persist. Those in Hebrews 11 saw the promises and embraced them though they never received them in the natural. That's where I'm going with this poem: what faith sees.

Faith sees the spring in your life.
Blossoms. Growth. Life. It's coming. It's coming.
Though snow's on the ground. You see?

FAITH vs. f.e.a.r.

Above all taking the shield of faith, wherewith ye shall be able to quench all the fiery darts of the wicked. (Ephesians 6:16)

Take your shield my brother
Grab your armor my sister
And fight the good fight of FAITH

f.e.a.r.
(False
Evidence
Appearing
Real)
is one of those hurtful darts
Used by the enemy, satan
By the which he hopes to hinder, handicap, harm, or hurt
And even kill the elect of the **Lord JESUS**

(here is where the saint can laugh out loud because…)

Ye are of God, little children, and have overcome them because greater is he (he = Holy Spirit) *that is in you than he that is in the world*
(I John 4:4)

so

put on the whole armour of God, that ye may be able to stand against the wiles of the devil
(Ephesians 6:11)

and remember that

*The weapons we fight with are not the weapons of
the world. On the contrary they have divine power
to demolish stronghold*s (II Corinthians 10:4 NIV)

what are these weapons exactly???
The NAME OF JESUS
The BLOOD OF JESUS &
The WORD OF GOD

So be encouraged my brother
And be strong my sister
For JESUS says, *Fear thou not; for I am with thee:
Be not dismayed; for I am thy God. I will strengthen
thee; yea I will help thee; Yea I will uphold thee
with the right hand of my righteousness* (Isaiah
41:10)

Speak to yourself
With **JESUS** i CAN use these weapons wisely
With **JESUS** i CAN have FAITH
With **JESUS** i CAN TRUST GOD
With **JESUS** i CAN win!!!

For the Bible says…
*Nay in all these things we (*insert your name here*)
are more than conquerors through him that loved us*
(Romans 8:37)

Faith / When the Son Springs Forth

I'm waiting
Patient expectation
Yearning even
For my break
A break in the clouds
That cover the horizon of my life
A break from the troubles
that have persisted for years

I cry out,
"When will it end, Lord?"

Funny thing is
Though the clouds loom
I comfort myself with this one thing:
I know, I said I KNOW
The Son is still shining in my life
My tearful eyes cannot see it
But my faith does

Like Abraham's faith,
Which reckoned that God could raise Isaac from the
dead
Or Samson's faith,
Which caused the pillars to come down
I have this same faith…
That the words spoken over my life
Will come to pass
Faith that God's plan for me will be fulfilled
Faith that my change is coming…

I already feel the weather changing
The sky is not so dark anymore
And faith says,
"One day
One day soon
The Son will spring forth,
Radiant and beautiful,
Breaking the chain of clouds,
The grip of the cold,
And the sorrow in my soul."

I WILL HAVE TRIUMPHED over my trial
And I will walk
In the Light of the Son

The Gospel: The Power Of God Unto Salvation

Romans 1:16

Join me on a ride
Back to ancient times
We talking bout the past
Some say antiquity
When you ended the year with a "B" and a "C"
The latter representing the last name of Him who
came
And took the blame
Restored the lame
Undid man's fate past the father of Cain (*Romans
5:12,14-15)*
The only Man ever with sin-free blood
In His veins

I'm your tour guide
Sit back as I tell the story
Of how this God/man Jesus died
And rose unto glory

Back then capital punishment was worse than death
You might gasp in your breath
When you learn how life left
Or desired to run away
From its earth container
When these heinous acts were inflicted
On these, the convicted

I digress

Of the Lord's death, hear the remainder
A life begun in a manger
And begun to "end" as they bore nails in
His hands
Both of His feet
Of the pain Jesus felt
I cannot speak

He was sinless to the day
They strung Him up on the tree
High on Calvary
The blood flowed down His extremities
(it shoulda been you and me)
instead Jesus took the rap for man's sin
and did so willingly

the cost of sin is death *(Romans 6:23)*
yall hold on peep
the price He paid, He paid for all
His Love's just that deep

So as Christ hung like a criminal
Darkness covered the land *(Matthew 27:45-50)*
The Father had placed the sins of man
Upon His only Son, the true sacrificial Lamb

But indeed this Son was @ His peak
So the other sun the Father had to hide
Know you not that if the Son of Man be lifted up
He'll draw all men to himself *(John 12:32-35)*

This precious life He did give up

And relinquished it to man
Then Jesus ROSE FROM THE GRAVE
And LIVES today
To complete the plan

Of redemption for man
Who, through Christ, can
overcome the sin
That dwells within
the flesh you now see and feel
hell fire won't consume it
please believe, its real

…that your sin brings to u death (*Romans 6:23*)
so, while u have breath
choose life
the Way of this Christ
obey the 38th verse of Acts 2
THEN
let His Spirit work holiness in you

that when this life is done
and the next one begun
you'll have overcome
sin and death; a world plagued by satan

you'll have what he lost through rebellion:
LIFE
with God Almighty in heaven

In Jesus' name, Amen.

A Poet's Poem For Caterpillars

A Poet's Poem…
I looked at black poetry
& what did I see
tales about you
some about me
allegedly
But little about He

For within the stanzas, lines, and rhymes I've read
Of certain poets, alive and dead –
Phillis, Paul L., Langston, Gwen, and Sonia –
Who paint characters so familiar, they might
knowya
Coloreds
Negroes
Niggers
Blacks now
Our creativity, intelligence, strength, and know-
how we endurerd, persevered
While lassoed and chained yesterday
Yet today it's the same
With a diffr'nt name
As freedom bells ring-rang
4th day 7th month
a holiday they claim

I buff my glasses again
Take a 2nd view
But that's all I see
Of the goodness within you and me

Told by these poets
And that's only when I squint long enough to
behold it
After I sift through the
Pimpsplayersdrugscussingdepression
And celebrated debauchery
Portrayed as our reality

Maybe for you?
If so
I pray
You have an ear
to hear
And eyes
to see
My reality
A new life, just the King and me (*John 3:5; II*
Corinthians 2:17)

For (Caterpillars)
I write words that give life to the life I live
Abundant that is
As one of His kids
Much different from the one's they see –
Fellow black poets of history –
In contextuality

My reality – changed
The life I live aint the same
Neither am i…why?

Well i believed on the name

Of the Man who was slain
(not by establishment, to appease whites' disdain of
brownskins who came - 'untamed', in chains, to die
insane and in vain)
NO…

i believed on the real Lamb (*John 1:29*)
whose plan was to take a stand
then the fall
pay the price for us all (*Romans 6:23*)
His grace + our faith
To answer the call
& follow the Way of the Light
so tall
for you see the life you live is not yours at all:

you cus
you lie
have sex w/out her hand
you may drink, or smoke
medication is your plan

for deep down you know
the person of whom the poets write
the black man/woman –
strongdynamicamindsobright –
as the mirror gazes @ you
it shows a life void of life
suffocated by the cares of this world
and succumbing when the world ends…
or just your time on it

i digress
of my life was I speaking
how I became a new being
it was the Lord's provision
for all whose decision
is submission
to His Plan (*Acts 2:38*)
to save man
with His right hand
as He did me
& given of His Spirit and Mind (*Acts 2:4*)
another life changed –
slave made free
I was once the caterpillar
slimy, crawling on its belly
many moving feet; a frenzy
yet traveling not
Bound
to the constraints of this world –
greed, lust, other evils thereof –
NOW..
a butterfly
Sailing above the struggle for justice and meaning
that plagued those leading men & women
Looking instead to the Son-King
Whose warmth abides within
And to His treasures above…

His name? "Jesus!" they say.
He's written a poem of your life too.
Won't you read what He has to say? (show crowd a
Bible)

Foregone Conclusion?

Forgone conclusion
Or so they thought.
When they saw Him there,
Lifeless on a tree.
After they had bored long nails
In His hands and feet.
Here He was:
The alleged Christ of God
Jesus of Nazareth
Dead.
They had terminated this nuisance,
Put an end to the miracles, signs, and wonders.
A foregone conclusion
Or so they thought.

Inspired by satan,
they had beaten Him beyond recognition.
Spit in His face.
Plucked His beard.
Mocked Him.
It seemed that mercy had left "Christ".
The one who was supposed to be Messiah
The Savior
Now to the amazement of all, here He hung.
Jesus was dead…
and so were the hopes of His disciples.
Day 1, day 2 and He was still dead.
It seemed Christ had gone the way of
leaders before Him-
Judas of Galilee and Theudas

Like them He would be forgotten.
His "ministry" would come to nought…

a forgone conclusion,
or so they thought.

But oh my friend,
I tell you of a truth.
That the story was not yet complete.
For on the third day Christ performed His greatest
work.
Like Jonah and the whale
He rose in triumph.
Oh yes my friend
Jesus Christ got up out of the grave.
The Man of war conquered sin and death.
For it was not possible that He should be holden of
it.
God would not leave His soul in Hell
Nor suffer the Holy One to see corruption.

Oh yes,
Christ rose
With all power in His hand.
Just as He said He would.
And He lives today.

So the next time you find your hope is small,
Or you're at the end of your rope, like the disciples
were,
Know that this is the exact time when the Lord will
come in.

The Lord of Glory, to lift up your bowed down
head.
So just hold on my brother;
And don't give up my sister.
Cuz it's not over.
WHY?
Because, HE IS ABLE...
to do exceeding abundantly above all you can ask or
think,
to be what you need Him to be when you need Him
to be it.

The great I AM;
The Ancient of Days;
He who was, is, and is to come.
Bless His holy Name.
Bless Him, Bless Him, Bless Him
My God!
Worthy is the Lamb of God...
Slain from the foundation of the world.
Worthy, Worthy, Worthy
Come on, Holy is His name
Come on, bless Him with me
Come on, Come on, Come on...

TESTIPO'TRY #1

Knees bent,
palms sweaty and stomach empty
tired arms, a weary head
Gushing eyes that bled,
A worn spirit
Aside my bed...
A shadow of myself
and that
Was my 'favorite' position

I misspoke.
Out of necessity I knelt.
Fa-vor-ite?
how could I savor it?
As my heart hung from the noose,
The chair recently kicked aside
Along with my pride...

Because I went to my mother
Who implicitly sensed the gravity of
The hurt
And duly felt a corresponding pain
And though she was my rock
And though she found meaning in my caretaking
And in my well-being
This woman
Whose might and will, dwarf her size
whose compassion seemed superhuman
Though full of good intent and kind words,

'next time don't give your heart away so fast, love
hurts,'
was all she could muster.

I went to my brother.
And told him the tale
And though he took my side
And took my mistake as 'understandable'
And though his harsh words
reflected the anger
aroused by the connection
to the pain-
words born of the resent he expressed
before I could
words later exchanged for a softer tone of sarcasm
and forward-looking, lessons learned-
the darkness grew still
and the cavity
on the inside
became too large to bear

I even went to my friend
Let out bitter jeers
The reaction formation-
attempting to allay
the gloom within
with the light of laughter
and wanting to use the intellect
to form:
structure within the chaos
meaning within the confusion

*a foundation within the bottomless pit into which I
had fallen…*

There was, and is, only one Way.

*As the tears came
Fueling the storm that
Raged in my soul
And as the mind, body, and spirit are
One,
triumvirate
The body reflected the dysfunction.*

*And when I laid it down to sleep
It would toss itself about
As if bound by stormy waves
Until, fatigued by stomach-wrenching sobs
The convulsions subsided,
only for a moment
as the current of recollections
flooded my mind
And in this way, another night was lost*

*As food came, it
Though my stomach was hollow
And teeth strong
And palette varied-
would take nothing
knowing that bread and water
could not satiate
the present hunger*

As all seemed lost
With my holiness corrupted
There He was…
Through one of His shepherds
He laid down the plan,
which He first told David:
'Cast your burden onto the Lord, and He shall
sustain you;
He shall never permit the righteous to be moved
(Psalm 55:22).'
And in the darkness there was light
And the way was clear
He stretched out His hand
Reached to my prostrate form
Lifted my chin and told me 'be not afraid'
He wiped my tears, ministered to me
And then
by and by
the healing came-
My mouth could eat
And…
my body
could sleep
And…
my mind
could rest
And…
my spirit
could forgive
And…
my heart
could heal…

And the Word came to life:

'Be anxious for nothing, but in everything by prayer and supplication, with thanksgiving, let your requests be made known to God; and the peace of God, which surpasses all understanding will guard your hearts and minds through Christ Jesus (Phil 4:6-7).'

May this peace be with you.
In Jesus' name I pray,
Amen.

Repentance

He beckons unto you.
Won't you heed?
"Turn.
Turn!
Oh sinner.
Return to your first love,
dear saint.
Though your sins
be the color of
blood
when exposed to oxygen,
I can color them like cumulus clouds."

"Bound in trespasses,
Come.
Aliens from Me,
Come.
Strangers from the promises,
Come.
Fearful,
Come.
Liars,
Come.
Faithless,
Come.
When you become sick of yourself
And what you have become,
Come.
Whomsoever will, let him come.
Confess

and forsake.
Then I promise to forgive & cleanse you
Only come."

"My sons via creation and salvation…
COME.
That I might cancel
Your date with death,
Your rendezvous with wrath,
Your meeting with malevolence.
For My Kingdom is here.
Even as I said in My eternal Word.
Allow Me to apply
My sinless blood to your heart,
while your blood runs warm in your veins."

But it all starts
when you decide to turn
from the sin that dwells within
and the temptation that dwells without.
This is repentance.

<u>Salvation</u>

Today is the day of salvation
Now is the time
So gird up yourselves
All ye people
Bring a repentant heart
Humble and contrite spirit
And desperation
To the Lord Jesus

Pack your knapsack of cares
backpack of worries
or suitcase of burdens
and leave them at the Master's feet
go 'head, lighten your load

for His Spirit is heavy
spiritually
when the Spirit fills thee
you'll cry melodies
of Abba Father

then come to the rivers of Zion
for water baptism
"in Jesus' name"
they'll proclaim
as they submerge you
His power separates you from sin
You're a new creature
Born again
A new life with Christ to begin

Amen.

Acknowledgements

I want to thank everyone who made this book possible – family, friends, mentors, and foes. So as to not neglect anyone, I will avoid listing names. You all were used to help create experiences in my life that God used as "material" for this book. And finally, thank You Jesus for giving me this gift of writing and allowing me to share it with the world!
I love you all with the love of Jesus Christ!

Future Works

Be on the lookout for additional books under 3**P**: **PH** **P**entecostal **P**ublishing. See us on the web at 3p-phpentecostalpublishing.weebly.com or search for us on facebook for updates and release dates.

About The Author

Patrick Henry, M.A., M.A., LPC is a Chicago native and two-time graduate of Northwestern University, where he earned a Bachelor's degree in Psychology and a Masters degree in Counseling Psychology. Most recently, he has earned another Masters in Developmental Psychology from Loyola University Chicago. Patrick has written poetry for over 20 years, and has written solely Christian pieces since shortly after Jesus saved him in 2002. From 2002-2017, he attended Christ Temple Apostolic Faith Church in Chicago, IL where he served as a teacher in Sunday School and in D.R. Bell Bible College and as a drummer. Patrick currently attends Endtime Apostolic Christian Holiness Church.

In addition to writing Christian poetry and books, Patrick is a trained counselor, teacher, and preacher. He can be reached at 614-522-9624 or at patrickhenry238@yahoo.com.

www.ingramcontent.com/pod-product-compliance
Lightning Source LLC
LaVergne TN
LVHW021407080426
835508LV00020B/2482